COLOMBIA

Lago Agrio

za

ena

PERU

Quito, Oct. 20/95

ECUADOR
FROM ABOVE

JORGE JUAN ANHALZER

First edition
October, 1993

ISBN
9978-65-008-3

Design and Preprinting
GRAFITTI DISEÑO GRÁFICO

Color Separations
SEPCAN S.A.

Book Binding
BINMAX S.A.

Printing
IMPRENTA MARISCAL

Printed in Ecuador

ECUADOR
FROM ABOVE

JORGE JUAN ANHALZER

GUIAS DE MONTAÑAS
ANDES EDITORES

Introduction

The precursor to this book, as with the previous ones about mountains, jungles, or flora and fauna, was adventure. As one hikes to the summits of the Andes and sees the condors flying over the páramo, it is easy to envy the perfect trajectories they trace out in the sky. As the temptation to imitate them became irresistible we thought that an ultraligtht would be the best way of doing so. Giving in to the compelling impulse, we bought one, fitted it out, and learnt to fly in it. After several nervous, unsteady and even catastrophic flights, came the longed for confidence that allowed us to take our eyes off the ground for a moment, if only to carry on doing so through the lens of a camera. In this strange apparatus we travelled the entire country in all her three dimensions. At sea level we took off from the beaches at low tide, and at 20,000 feet we flew over Cotopaxi; although obviusly not in the same journey! Between these two extremes were the flights that took us over the rainforests, the rivers, the villages and the fields of a country that, although small, is enormously varied, not only in the different levels of elevation, but in every possible sense.

The ultralight, baptized somewhat maliciously as "the Vengeful Vulture" by the neighborhood, was not only the cheapest way of undertaking a project of this sort, but also the most practical. There was not the problem of waiting patiently for a combination of good weather and pilot availability. Nor did we face the obstacle we had experienced previously when flying in helicopters or small aircraft, whereby the pilot usually does not understand what one wants in terms of precise angles, partly because often the photographer himself does not know. Another advantage afforded us by "the vulture" was that it has neither a cabin nor windows, which in airplanes tend to be scratched and opaque. Because of this the view is as clear and uninterrupted as the weather itself permits. On the other hand, this absence of a cabin was a disadvantage when flying at high altitudes - Imagine how cold it was!

Above all, however, what "the vulture" gave us was the great pleasure that invariably comes with adventure. We flew high in the air, the wind blasting our faces, with nothing between ourselves and the sky. (Of course, there was also not much between ourselves and the ground!). We were able to travel over the native landscape with the freedom of a bird, paying no heed to the obstacles that mountains, precipices, rivers, or private property normally place between oneself and ones dreams. In this machine we were not restricted by roads and paths, nor hindered by the whims of their curves.

Flying over farms and fields we were met by the aroma of coffee, the smell of stables and the stench of carrion. Smelling what the vultures smell made us feel even more like birds. When, at several meters from the ground, we turned off the engine in order to glide our way down, sounds of every description were brought to us on the breeze: the waves as they broke on the beach three hundred feet below us; the enticing offers of the street vendors; and the erratic yelps of a restless dog. In other words, we simulated as close as is humanly possible the flight of a bird. Once or twice a defiant hawk or a cautious frigate approached us for a moment to fly by our side. For a minute or two we tried to imitate them. If they veered to the right or the left we did the same. But invariably they would turn abruptly and disappear from sight, leaving us in no doubt as to who are the experts.

The above paragraphs are written in the plural because "the vulture" is a two seater. the passenger seat has, at some time or another, been occupied by almost every member of my family, many friends, and several curious onlookers who, in the different places in which we landed, approached us with such genuine surprise that there was nothing for it but to take them for a spin! The ages of the copilots ranges from the smallest of my children who went up in my wife's arms when he was only two, to my great aunt who flew at the age of eighty-six. These shared aventures have evoked a wide variety of commentaries. One black Esmeraldas man, after his flight at barely a hundred feet from the ground, turned purple despite his natural color. He insisted that this was not due to fright but to the cold that he felt up there, and that after such an experience he no longer wished to know Quito (the capital that is at 9,000 feet above sea level) where, according to him, it must be at least as cold! Then there was the young country boy who asked why it was that from the air he had seen ants that looked somewhat like cows, but from the ground he could only see cows and not ants.

Apart from the often blindly trusting and invariably naive companion, the official copilot, with whom I confronted the more risky flights, such as the one that took us across the Andes, was Romulo Cardenas who seems to derive intense enjoyment from adventure. We also travelled, on several ocassions, with two or even three ultralights flying together.

After this experience one can say that Ecuador as seen from the air looks almost entirely green. The virgin jungles, the forests and the fields knit a green blanket that covers almost everything. That which is not actually green in color is usually "greenery" none the less. If the bananas and palm trees are sometimes yellow, for example, it is only because something is wrong with the pest control. And if the wheat and corn are the same color it is because they are already ripe.

Interrupting this green landscape are the desert areas which, although few, are unfortunately getting more and more severe every day. The heights of the Andes also provide contrast, their slopes being brown and their highest summits, covered in snow and ice, being entirely white. But the moorlands and glaciers occupy relatively little of Ecuador's surface. It is worth pointing out that, although on maps the mountain range is always depicted as wide and brown, in reality most of its surface, the outer slopes as much as in the inter-andean valleys, are mostly green.

In the countryside the only things to interrupt the greenery are the little houses that splatter the landscape with white dots. In the cities and towns, on the other hand, it is the dots that are green, the parks and gardens breaking up what is otherwise seen as a expanse of white.

But not everything is monochrome. The wild "Arupos" flower purple, the Kapok trees sprout white flowers, and the "Guayacanes" bloom yellow. The rivers can also be distinguished by the color of their waters. Those of the mountains are white with foam, whilst further down they become transparent blue. Finally, as they enter the lowlands, they adopt the colors and shape of a gigantic boa: brown and undulating. The rivers born in the depths of the jungle are dark black but in the light of the sun they glisten like silver.

The photographs that comprise the following work are not separated by regions, which is how the country is often devided in matters of culture, science, sport and politics. With the idea that Ecuador, although diverse, is a single nation, we have grouped the photographs more by way of the theme they represent than by the places in which they were taken.

The reader will have to excuse the fact that we have not been able to identify all the crops depicted in these photographs. It would would have been time comsuming and risky to land in every place of which a picture was taken in order to find out what was going on. Time consuming because there are many of them, and risky because it is highly likely that not all of the farmers would have been happy to have their fields invaded by a flying object of dubious identity.

Having shared the ideas and interests that lay behind the making of it, I now present the results of this work.

HC-ALN

MX
II

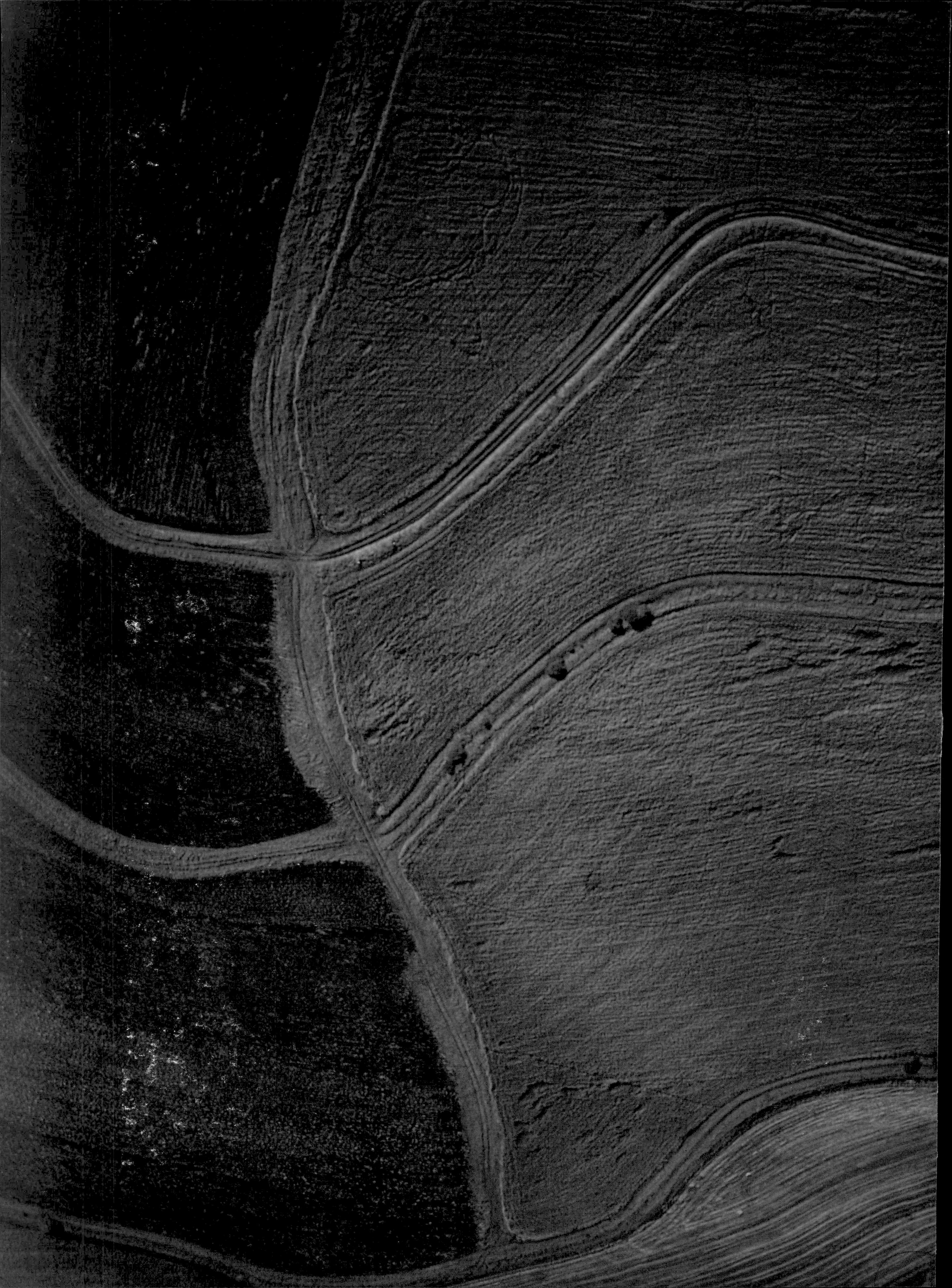

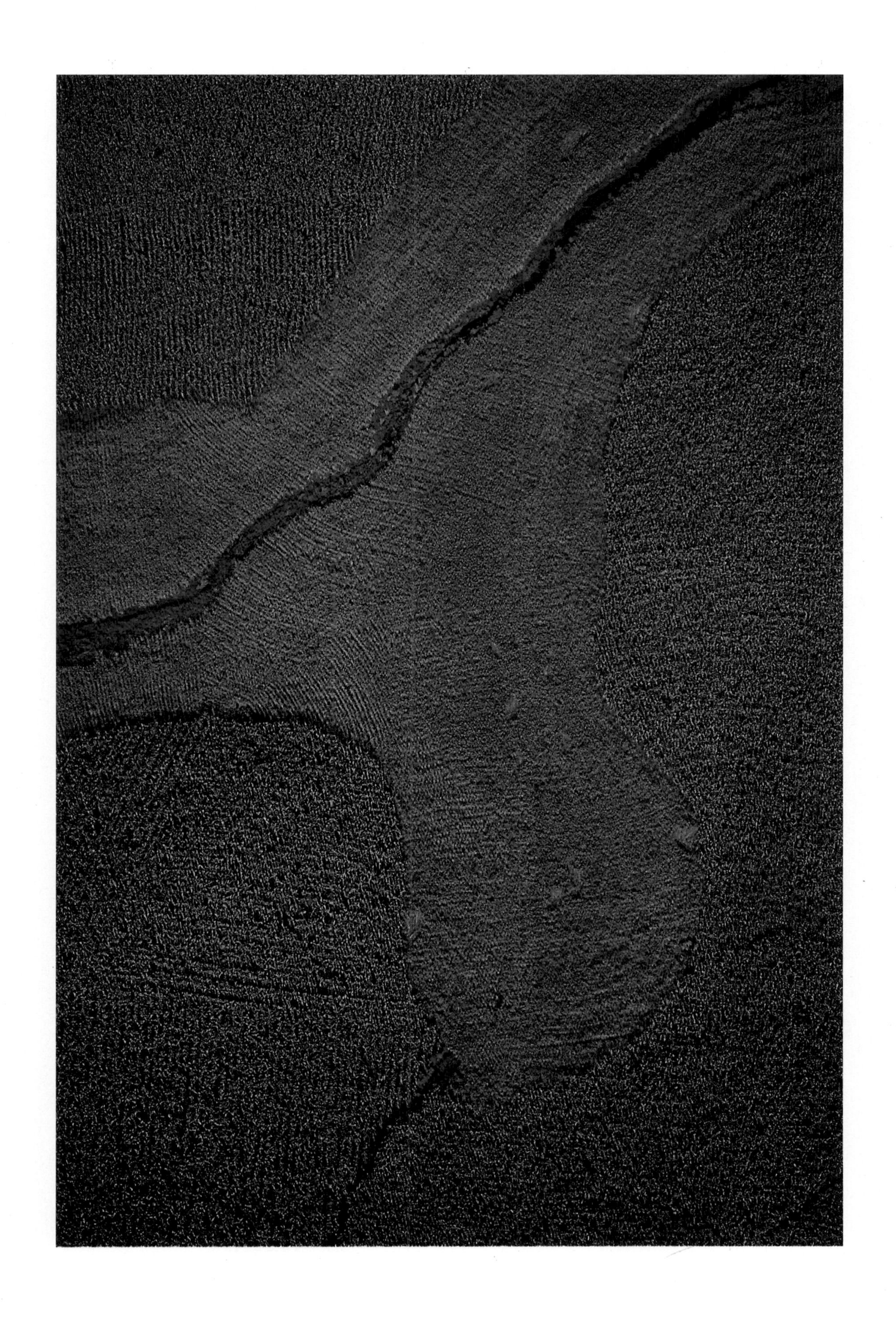

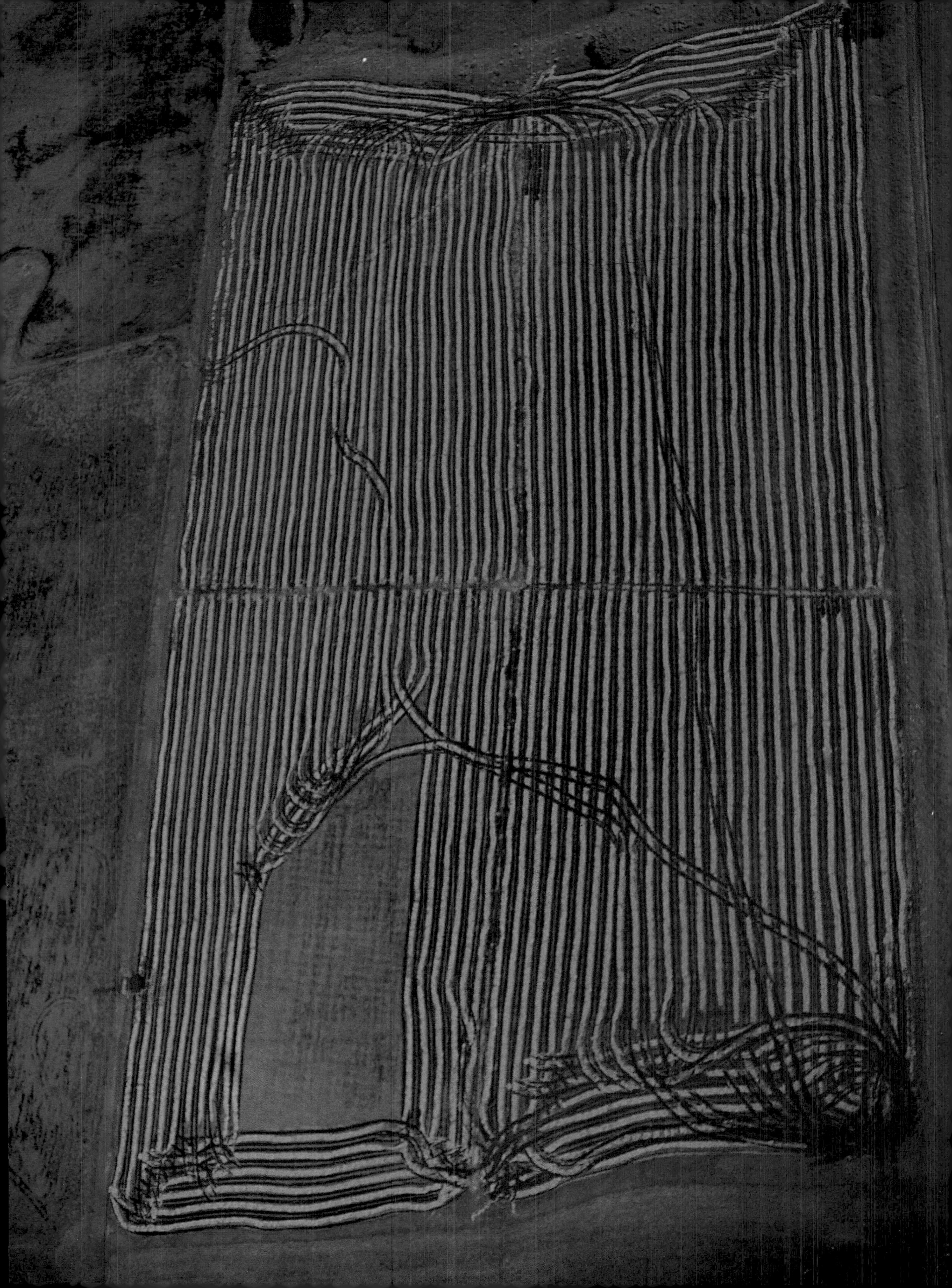

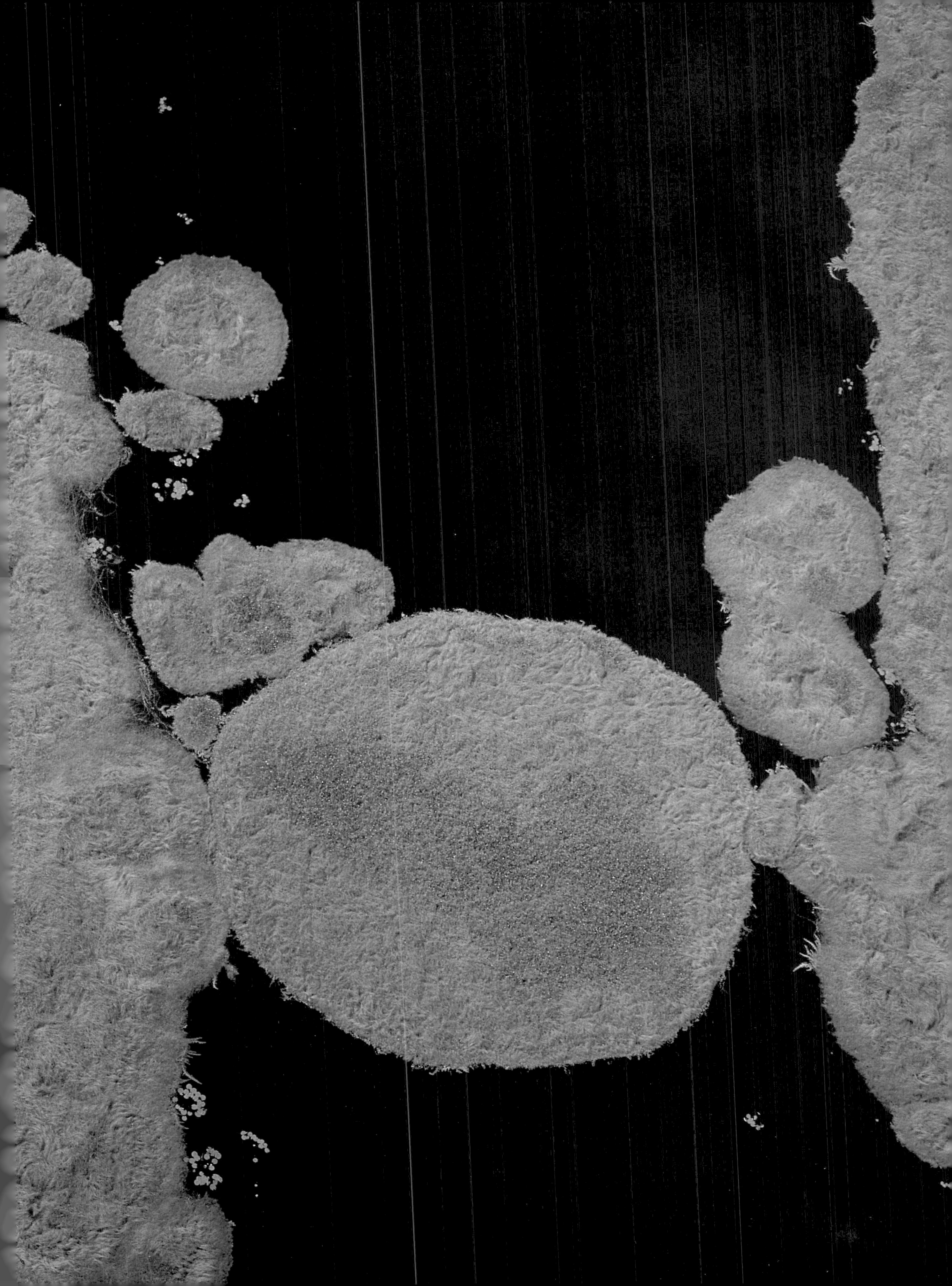

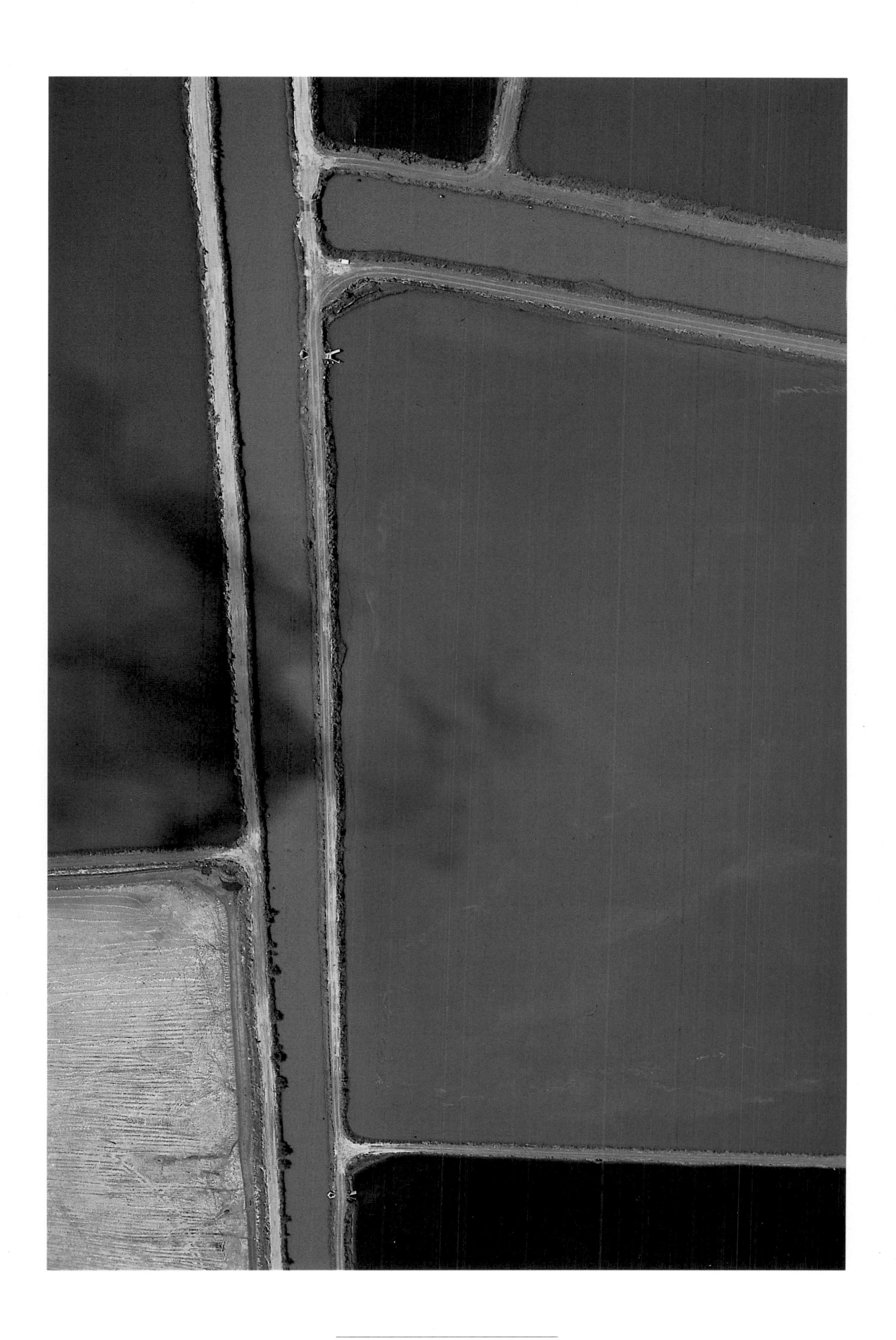

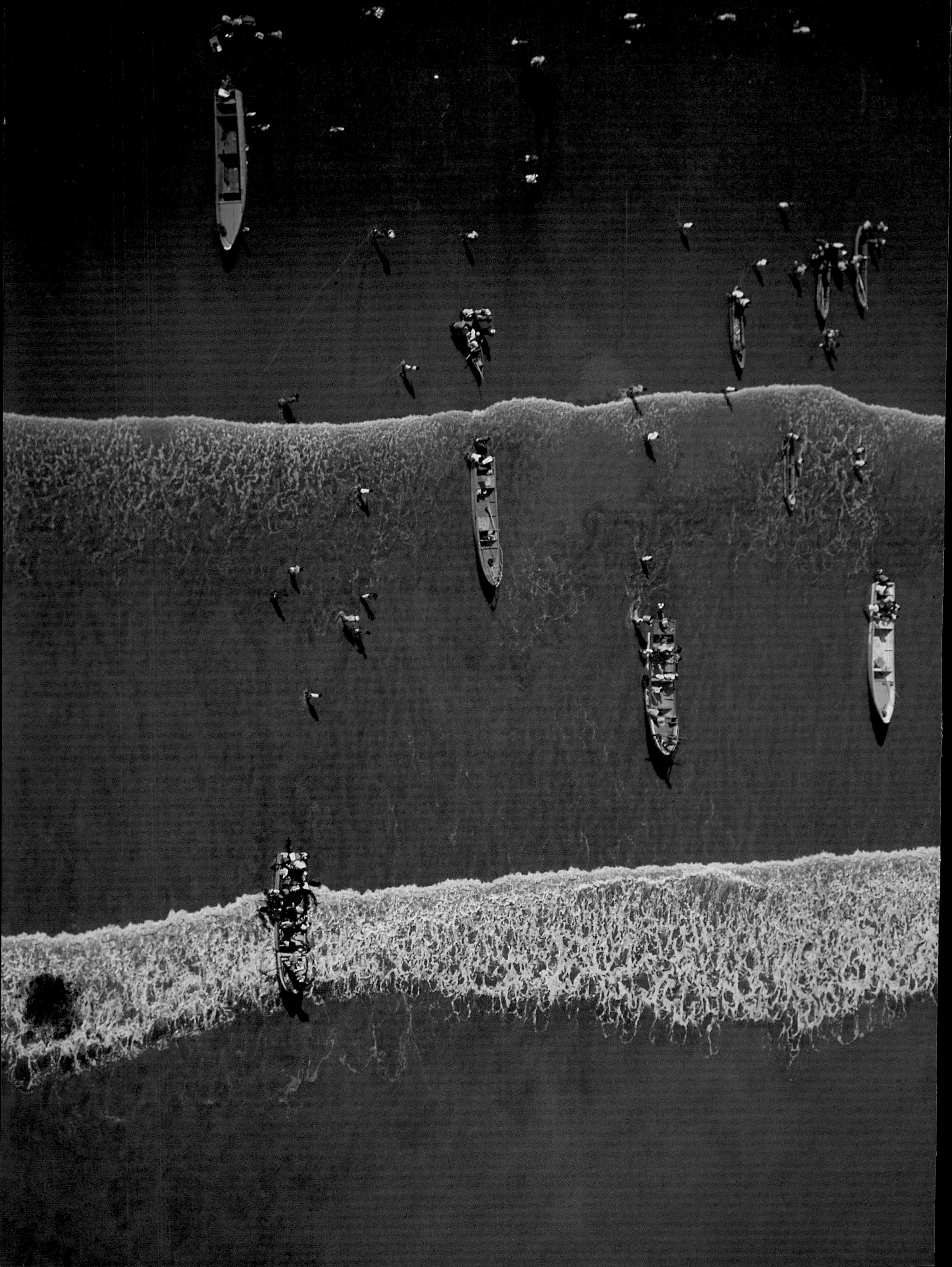

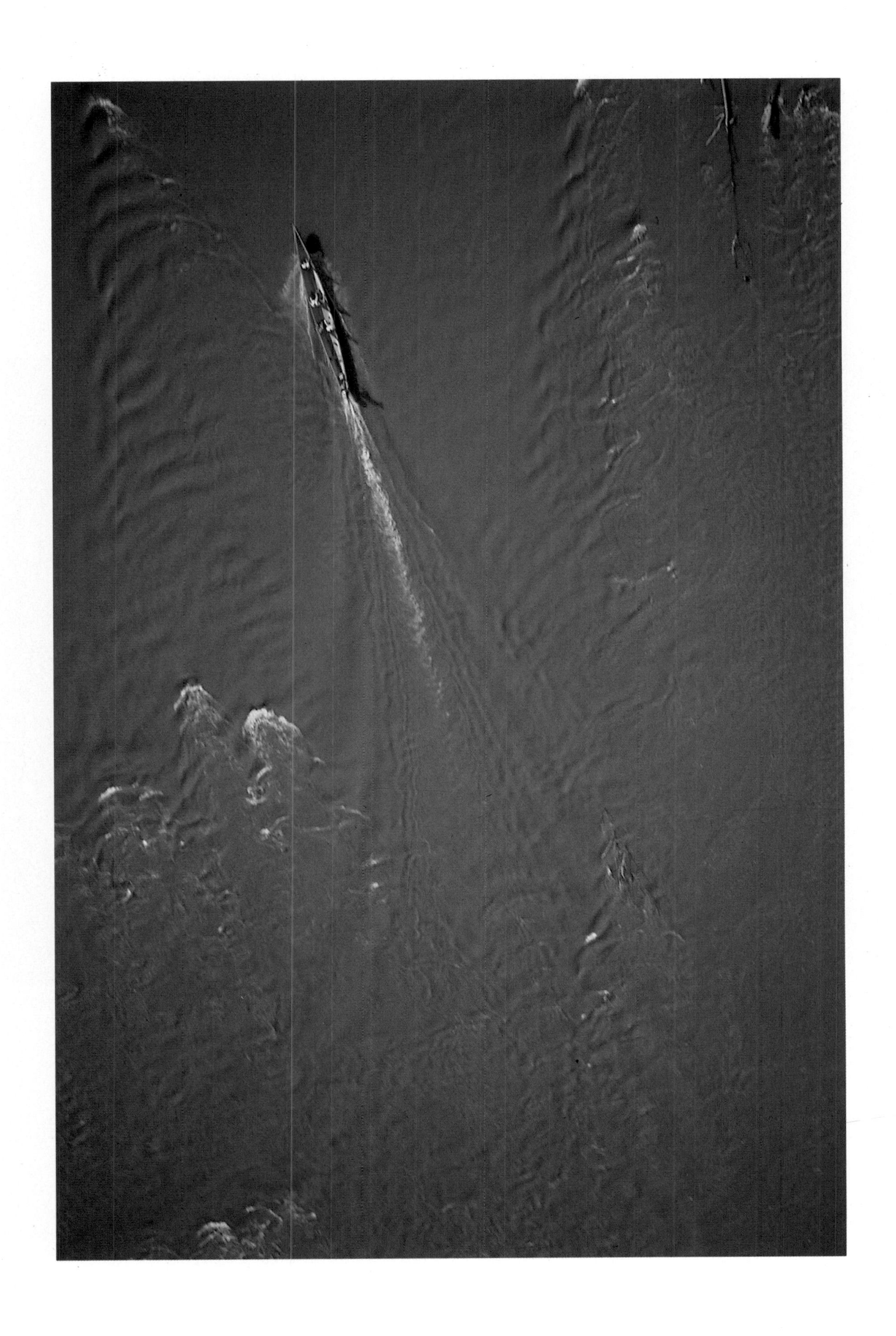

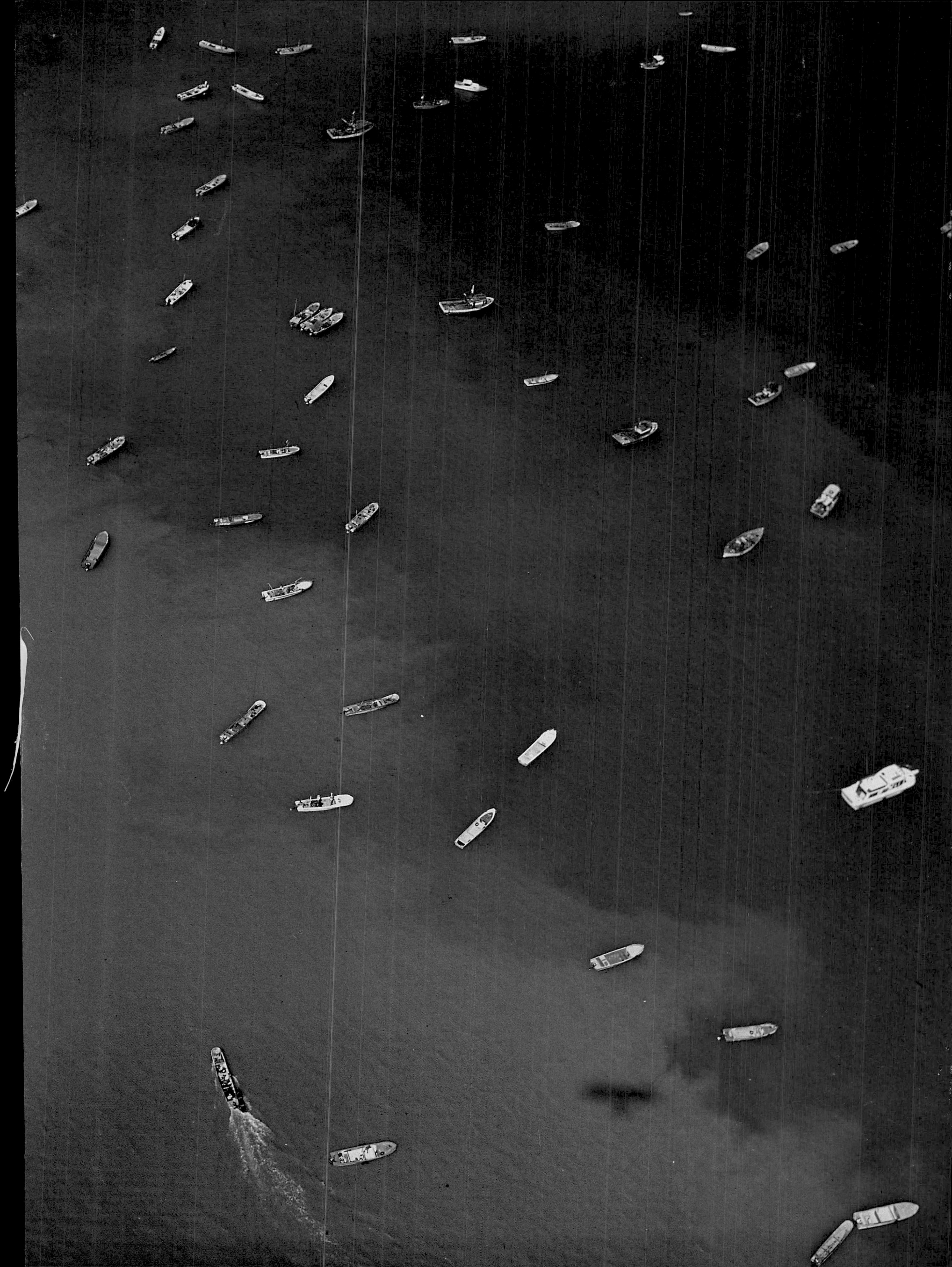

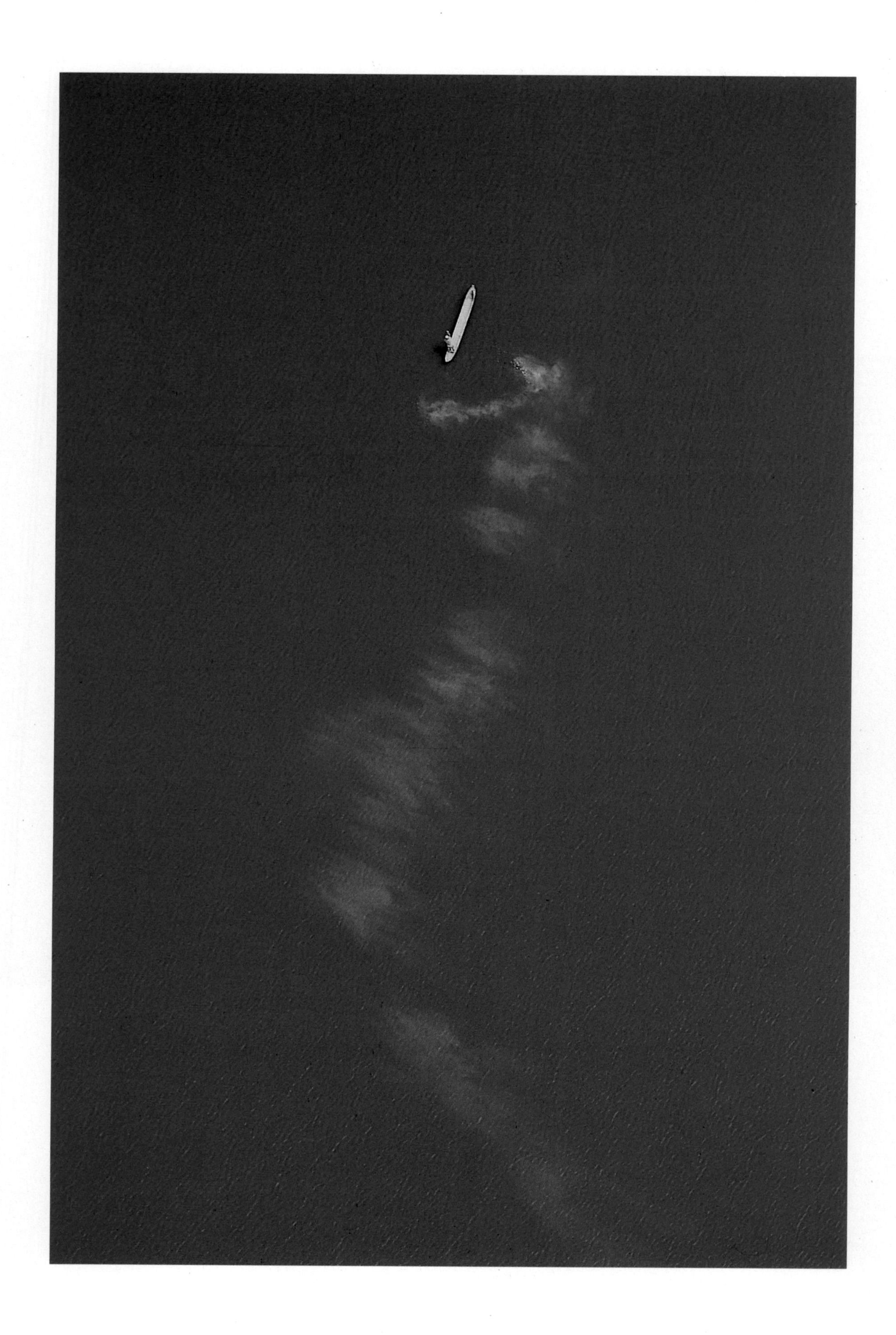

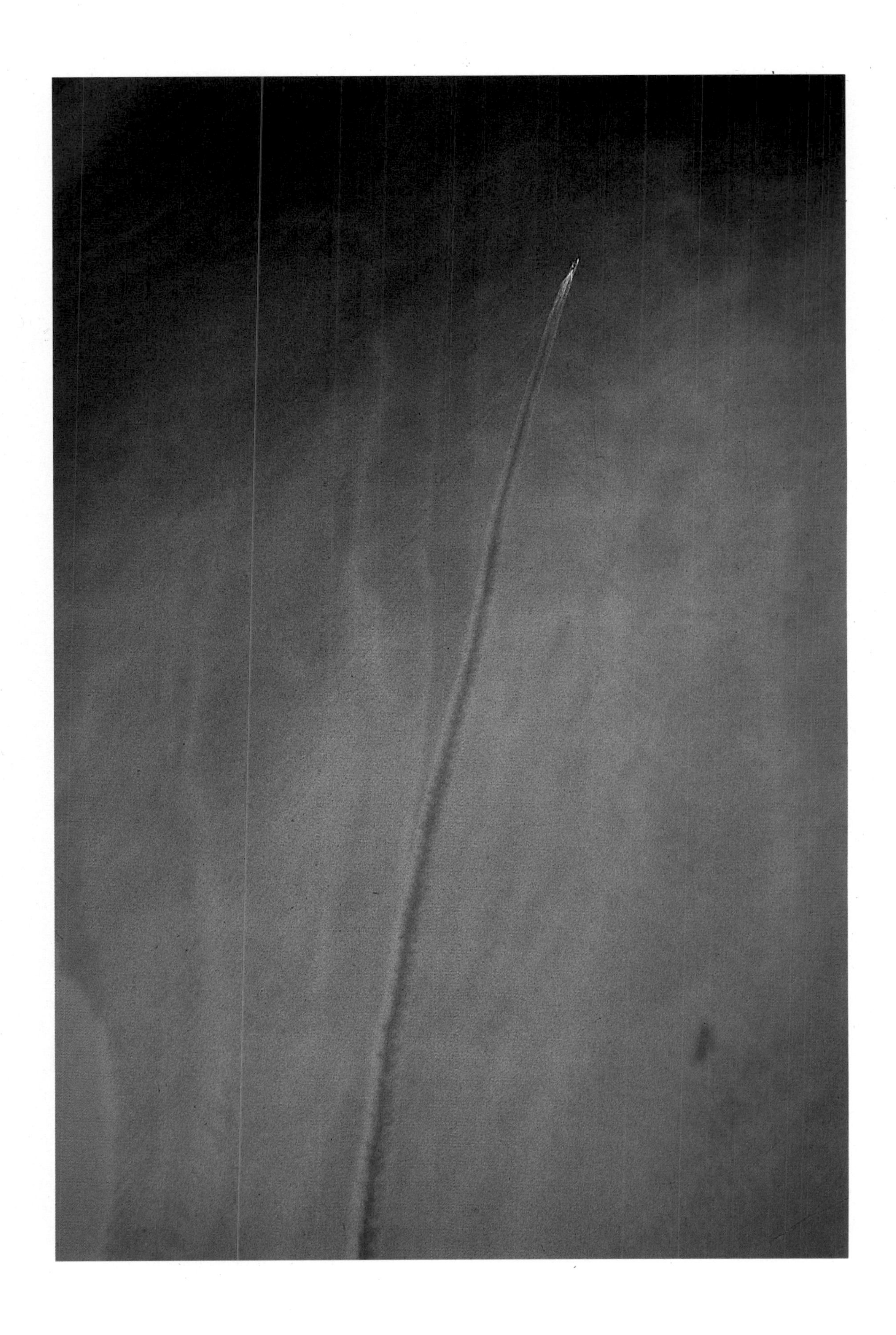

Photographic introduction

5. MACHALILLA
The hand is not only pointing out the boats anchored opposite the village of Machalilla, but is also inviting one to share a unique vision of Ecuador, reserved until now for the birds and a limited number of aviators.

6-7. QUITO
Quito is located in a long and narrow valley, at the foot of the Pichincha volcano. The continuity of the city is broken by a hill called Panecillo, meaning in spanish the little bread loaf.

8-9. THE ILINIZAS
Following a heavy storm and beneath a sky that forecasts more snow, the Ilinizas emerge. The southern one is on the left, the northern one on the right.

10-11. MOJANDA
The slopes of Mojanda, 13,900 feet, are like a chess board painted by a reckless child and crumpled by the whim of geology.

12-13. THE HEIGHTS OF TANDAPI
As they descend towards the coast, the Andes are a chaotic tangle of ridges and ravines. The jungle clambers up them, reaching over twelve thousand feet above sea level.

14-15. BALZAR
Balzar is situated on a bend of the river Daule. The city prospers not only because it has a river but because it is situated between the biggest stretch of rice fields in the country and the land where maize and soy beans are grown.

16-17. THE PLAYITA
Fortunately for the adventurous there are still a few beaches to which one can only get by boat or on foot. One can even land on a few of them.

18. ABOVE MANABI
Flying over the Crespa mountains we reached Chone, one of the many journeys made to photograph the country.

22. CAYAMBE
While the dawn mist covers the dim valleys, the summit of Cayambe has long been warmed by the sun.

23. NORTHERN ILINIZA
A heavy winter snowfall has covered the slopes of the northern peak of the Ilinizas. In the darkness of the background we can just make out the lowlands of the coast.

24-25. COTOPAXI
A group of startled mountaineers pose in line on the summit of Cotopaxi. At 19,700 feet this volcano is the second highest peak in Ecuador after Chimborazo.

26. ANTIZANA
Conceptually polarized but close on singular occasions, jungle and snow hold hands on the eastern slopes of Antizana.

27. SOUTHERN ILINIZA
The steep slopes of Iliniza are topped with a lenticular cloud maintained at the side of the summit by rotor winds. Chimborazo appears in the background..

28-29. ANTIZANA
Broken glaciers slide down from the four summits of Antizana, feeding the rivers of the Amazonia as they melt. In the distance we can see Cayambe Volcano.

30. COTOPAXI
In the dawn following a heavy snowfall, Cotopaxi emerges completely white, the access route drawing a zigzag up the mountain side. The cars that climb this road reach 15,000 feet above sea level.

31. SINCHOLAGUA
The majority of the elevations in the country are of volcanic origin. Many of them, like Sincholagua, ceased being active a long time ago, and with the passing of the milleniums erosion has carved new shapes in their summits.

32. LA ESPERANZA
At the foot of the Mojanda inactive volcano lies the town of La Esperanza, it is build in the spanish way with the church and the local goverment around a central square.

33. PASOCHOA
The skirts of Pasochoa are patterned with meadows, cornfields and eucalyptus forests. Her 13,800 feet summit can be made out in the distance.

34. COCHASQUI
The truncated pyramids of Cochasquí are found on the southern slopes of Mojanda. They were built by the Caras, a civilization that preceded the Incas. The ruins occupy a privileged position from where you can see Cotopaxi, Antizana and Cayambe, as well as all the smaller mountains of the region.

35. CUICOCHA
According to legend, Imbabura is a charming Don Juan to the peasant girls who graze their flocks at its feet. But its heart is taken by Cotacachi. Cuicocha, the lake nestled within her skirts, is an open wound caused by the wrath of the jealous and passionate Imbabura.

36. SALINAS OF IMBABURA
Until recently, in the times before industrially produced salt, the salty soil in Salinas used to be washed to obtain this mineral. Small mounds of earth, the remains of this ancient technique, lie sprinkled across the valley.

37. ATUNTAQUI
In the countryside the land is generally divided into farms or small plots. The communal small holdings in the areas of high indigenous population are generally "huasipungos" granted to the peasants in the times of the agrarian reform.

38-39. SAN PABLO LAKE AND MT. IMBABURA
With its height and ancient magic, Imbabura dominates the surrounding valley and influences the souls of its inhabitants, the industrious Otavalenians.

40. TATATAMBO
With the mountain above and the precipice below, the road which unites the mountain valleys (Aloag) with the coastal plains (Santo Domingo) has no choice but to imitate the river Santa Ana situated at the foot of the face, snaking its way down the mountain.

41. THE GUACAMAYOS MOUNTAIN RANGE
This is how all the slopes of the Andes used to look, covered in Cloud Forest. These days settlers' farms replace them. There are few original forests remaining on the western slopes, and on the eastern ones they are only slightly more extensive.

42-43. REVENTADOR
Surrounded and almost covered by the forest, the young volcanoes rise eastward of the great cordillera. Many years will have to pass by, and a greater number of eruptions will have to spew out of their mouths, in order for them to acquire the white glaciated heads of their older brothers.

44. THE SKIRTS OF QUININDE
On cloudy days, when the banana leaves are open and thus better disposed to receive chemical, the plants are fumigated against the various diseases to which the are prone.

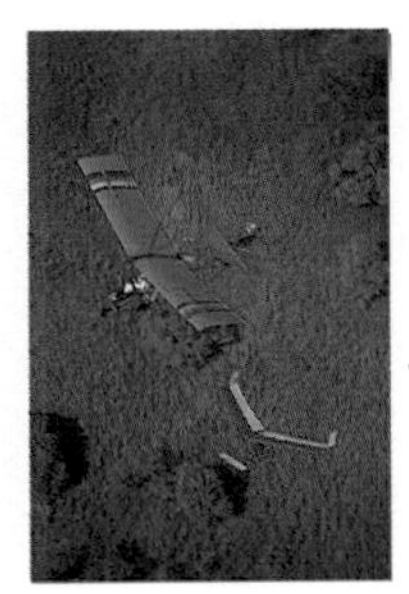

45. OVER GUAYAS
On several occasions we were accompanied throughout our journey by other ultralights.

46. SKIRTS OF QUEVEDO
A column of smoke produced by the burning of weeds rises up towards the sky. This is how the peasants do away with the plants that compete with their maize crops.

47. FUMISA
"Second to none", the ecuadorian banana farmers proudly claim when talking about their product. This fruit is the second most important export commodity after oil.

48. THE SKIRTS OF MOJANDA
In the middle of a cultivation that is difficult to identify, there is a construction that serves as nothing more than a temporary shelter for the person who looks after the crop. The houses in which the families actually live at least have a small patio.

49. LA VICTORIA
A little bit of everything is sown in this valley. The rows are maracuya bushes, and the golden crops are maize. Between the trees are rows of bananas, coffee and cacao, and even the river is covered by some kind of plant. The rest of the crops are sufficiently unrecognizable as not to risk an opinion.

50-51. CONGUILLO
Straight borders, ignoring geographical contours, divide up the plots of the smallholders. By the looks of things each proprietor has a different idea as to what should be sown.

52. MOCHA
The furrows in which the potatoes are planted are wavy because they follow countour lines for plowing. This technique avoids soil erosion, but is unfortunately seldom used in the country.

53. THE OUTSKIRTS OF PATRICIA PILAR
In the middle of a maracuya plantation stands a small house, true to the traditional style of coastal architecture. It is built on stilts so that the breeze can ventilate it, the walls are made of guadua cane and the roof of bijao leaves.

54. PUJILI
In the last months of every year the land goes under the plough, it will take a couple of months for the rain to green the landscape again.

55. LASSO
The sourrounding areas of the active volcanoes are made of sandy ground. As soon as the rains stop, the ground dries as the water easily percolates through, water surfaces again kilometers downstream in springs, many of them hot due to the proximity of the volcanoes.

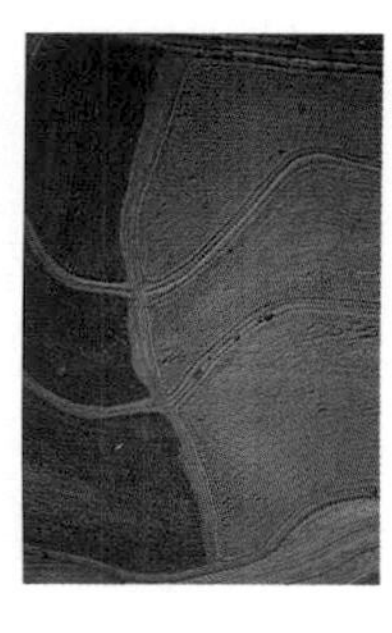

56. CUTUGLAGUA
Here the life cycle of the wheat crop can be seen in its two extremes. On one side the ears, golden before the harvest, and on the other, the top soil prepared for the next sowing.

57. CUTUGLAGUA
These small fields, in which they are experimenting with wheat, look like a close up photograph showing the texture of the threads of a piece of fabric.

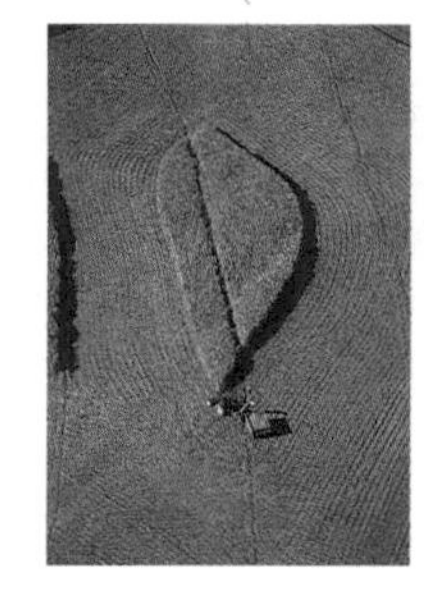

58. SALINAS OF IMBABURA
This sunflower crop, harvested by a tractor, will serve as cattle fodder, although this plant is usually used for the extraction of a fine, edible oil.

59. SALCEDO
The dairy farmers in Ecuador need not to worry about crude winters or suffocating summers, the country mild differences between seasons are a couple of months of sligthly drier and windy weather.

60. EL ANGEL
In the mountainous areas the soil is plowed during the dry months from July to September. When the rains come in October the sowing begins.

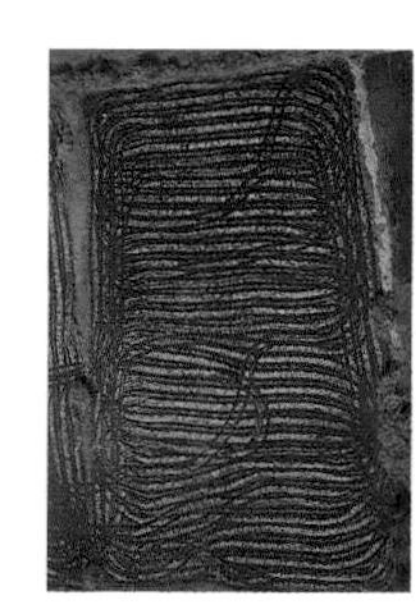

61. SANTA LUCIA
The numerous turns of the rice harvester create an abstract painting in the muddy field.

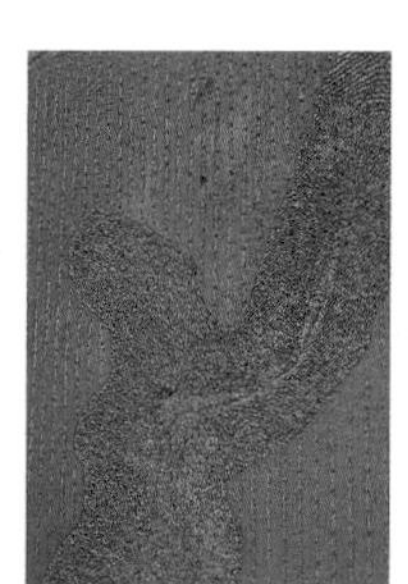

62. LA CONCORDIA
A palm oil cultivator has planted maize amongst the palm next to the stream, and soya beans amongst the palm on the plain.

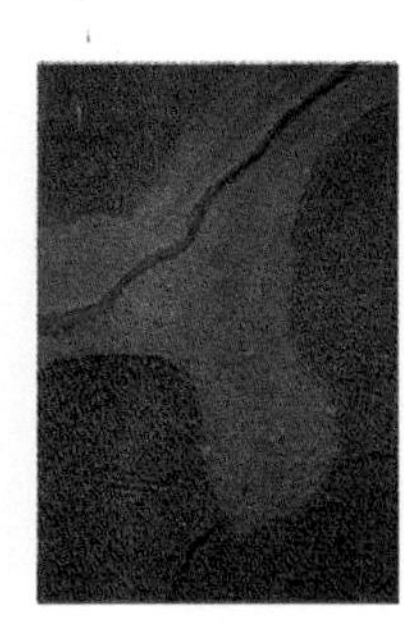

63. MOCACHE
Another farmer dedicated to the sowing of maize (yellow) has not managed to conquer the swampy bed of a small stream (green).

64. EL CARMEN
The geometric design of the nurseries is of debatable perfection, whereas the left-overs of the jungle look chaotic.

65. SANTA LUCIA
The rice straw that remains between the tracks left behind by the combine harvester in the dark mud, is yellow, whilst the cereal not yet collected is green.

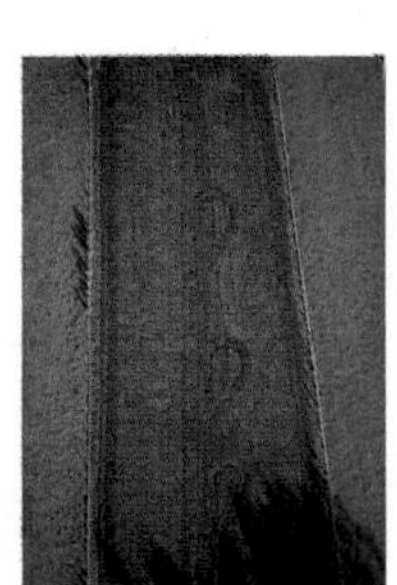

66. TAMBILLO
The valleys of Ecuador´s Andean spine produce mainly milk, sweetcorn, and vegetables. Most of the land is dedicated to pasture to feed the cattle.

67. ALOAG
Unaware of their art, the tractor drivers who plow the fields make innumerable turns in the earth. Rousseau mentioned, although in a different sense, that agriculture is the most noble of the arts.

68. SANTA LUCIA
The land bordering Santa Lucia lies low and flat, flooding each year with the winter rains. With the advantage provided by these natural circumstances, it is here that enough rice to support the whole country is produced. In good years there is even enough surplus for export.

69. SANTA LUCIA
The thin, wavy lines are dykes of earth, built to contain the water inside the shallow rice paddies.

70-71. LAS HERRERIAS
The great farm houses are the lega cy from colonial times. They can be found scattered through the valleys sorrounding Quito. They were built by landlords and most of them belong today to their descendants.

72. EL CARMEN
The fertility of the ground in the andean valleys is quite high. All the valleys are sorrounded by volcanoes that through the years have covered the land with millons of tons of minerals.

73. TILIPULO
Many of these "hacienda" houses were surrounded by huge estates: some pasture and agricultural land, but mostly moorelands and jungles. As the house was the only building around, it usually has a church within, a storage facility, place for some manufacturing and even a foodstore.

74. THE OUTSKIRTS OF LATACUNGA
Escaped from the barn, the cows are fast on their way towards an alfalfa patch. The cow keeper problably went through a bad time as the cows become bloated easily after eating fresh alfalfa.

75. BABAHOYO
On the coastal plains and, to a lesser extent, on those of the Amazon basin which is still mainly primary forest, tropical breeds of cattle such as the brahman or the cebu are raised.

76. AFRICAN PALM
It is best for farmers if the land is flat, but it does not appear to matter too much if it is not, as we can see from this african palm plantation.

77. LA MINGA
The tradition of the "mingas" survives from precolumbian times, takes place when all the neighbors give a hand to the one of them in need of help. In this way houses are made, churches, roads, or irrigation canals. Needless to say that the "mingas" usually end in a big celebration.

78. THE SKIRTS OF COTACACHI
Sourrounded by a crop of ripe sugar cane, which looks as though it was planted with a comb, stands a little house made of "adobe" and tiles. The yellow border belongs to a plot of ripe maize cane.

79. DAULE-PERIPA
A handful of trees, wilted from so much water, stand surrounded by weeds and with their roots submerged in the water of the biggest dam in the country.

80. WESTERN SLOPES OF THE ANDES
Unpleasant but common, the views of the mountain clearings serve as a sharp reminder that, of the original primary forest in the west of the country, barely 6% remains.

81. ZANCUDO
The monotony of the green canopy is only broken ocasionally by the flowering trees (not counting of course human activities). Some trees flower purple while others become red, yellow or white.

82. CHOTA
The Chota valley is set in a mini-desert; not the only one in Ecuador but perhaps the most extreme. Along the length of the Andes, the green valleys alternate with the dry ones.

83. CHOTA
Eroded by the wind and toasted by the sun, the slopes of the Chota valley are a desert where the few things that grow serve as food for the goats of the valley´s black inhabitants.

85. TABACUNDO
In the light of the dawn, the shadows of several eucalyptus and a couple of pine trees stretch out across the mist and maize plantations.

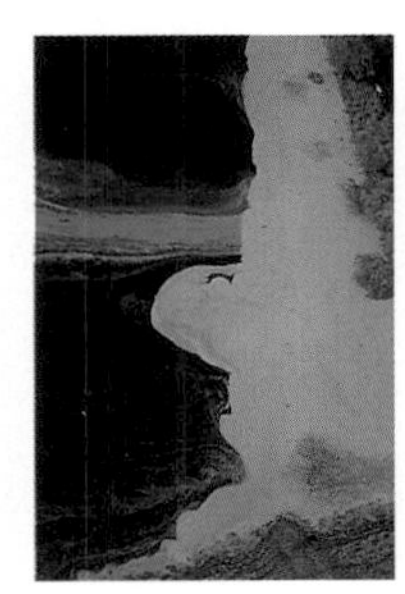

86. ATACAMES
Black water, green algae and a lifeless tree in their midst, create a strange landscape in a swamp near the sea.

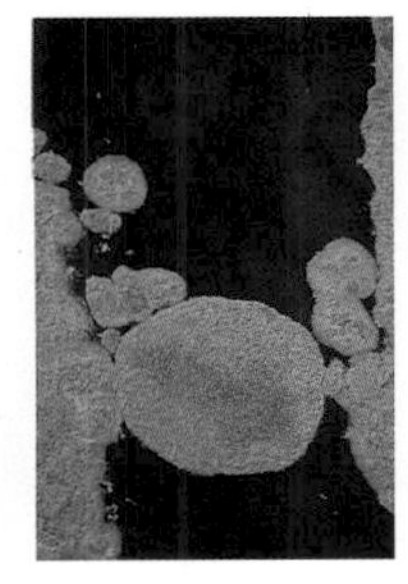

87. VINCES
Clouds are reflected on the surface of a lake with murky water and floating islands.

88. BABAHOYO
Sunset reflects in the rice paddies of the low flatlands, in the rainy season the rivers flood the plains thus giving a helping hand to the farmers.

89. SAME
Not far from the beaches of Same is a forest surrounded by a swamp. This area is a sanctuary for sea birds.

90-91 GUAYAQUIL
On the mouth of the Guayas river rises the biggest city of Ecuador, With two million inhabitants it has also the biggest economy. It is as well one of the most important ports of the Pacific.

92. TONCHIHUE
The plots most sought after for the shrimp beds are those which are close to the sea, but which also have access to the freshwater of a river. This is because different saline intensities are needed during the various different stages of the shrimps' growth.

93. MUISNE
The excessive felling of mangroves for the installation of pools where shrimps grow in captivity has created many problems. The traditional fishermen now have nothing to fish, and the shrimp farmers themselves now have difficulties obtaining larvae as it was precisely within the mangroves that the crustaceans used to reproduce.

94. SAN JACINTO
Where once there were mangroves there are now shrimp beds, our diet and economy dependent on the risky promise of a monoculture crop.

95. RIVER MOUTH OF THE BRICEÑO
Not all the shrimp beds belong to large companies. Some of the village suburbs have small pools, each with a separate owner.

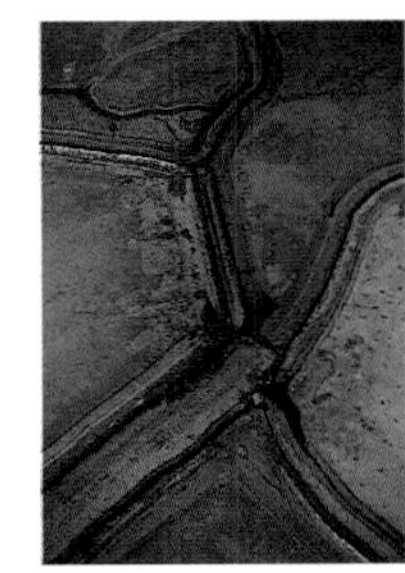

96. PEDERNALES
Solitary amongst the empty pools stands the building which houses the pumps used to suction river or sea water.

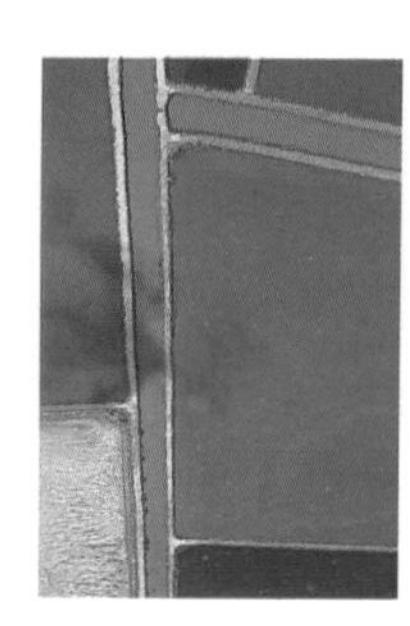

97. RIVER CHONE ESTUARY
The shrimp beds are many different colors. It is probably the different depths and saline intensities of the waters that are responsible for giving each pool a distinct hue.

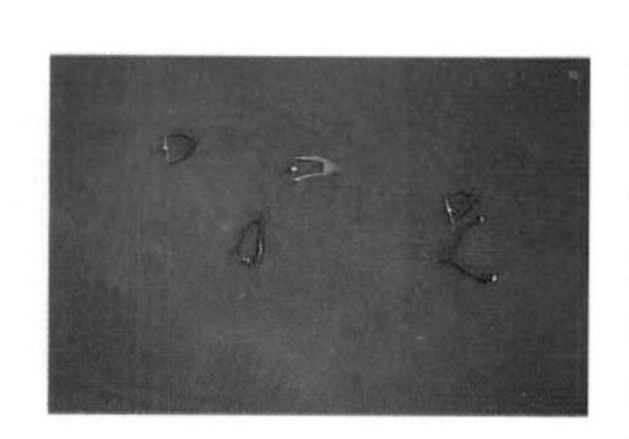

98-99. MAL PELO
The 'larveros' are people from inland who camp on the beach during periods of either a waxing or waning moon. Under these particular lunar conditions, at high tide, they sieve the waves with red nets. They sell the shrimp larvae to the laboratories.

100-101. THE FRAILES
One part cliff, another of sand, and a third of mountain vegetation form the horseshoe shape of this beach, one of the prettiest in the country.

102. PUNTA CANGREJO
Whatever is high and hard near the shoreline becomes with time either a point or a cape, elsewhere (beside the mangrovees in the estuaries, where actually the land gains territory) the sea erodes the coast at a faster rate.

103. GALERA POINT
In the south of Esmeraldas, at Galera point, the mainland dips into the sea. Today a lighthouse aids navigation, but there are some who search for the remains of several Spanish galleons shipwrecked during the colonial era, along with the treasures they probably carried.

104 COJIMIES ESTUARY
The Cojimies river gets tangled with the sea in an embrace of chanels and islands, all this chaos creates powerfull currents respected by the boat people that transport the shrimps from the many farms that lay there in.

105. THE SEA IN MANGLAR ALTO
The waves that break on the beaches of Ecuador cross the Pacific interrupted only by the Galapagos.

106. SAME
As the sun goes down a bongo sets out to sea. In the darkness of the night the fishermen cast their nets in the hope of catching shrimp and fishwhich, at the late hour, feed on the surface of the wat.

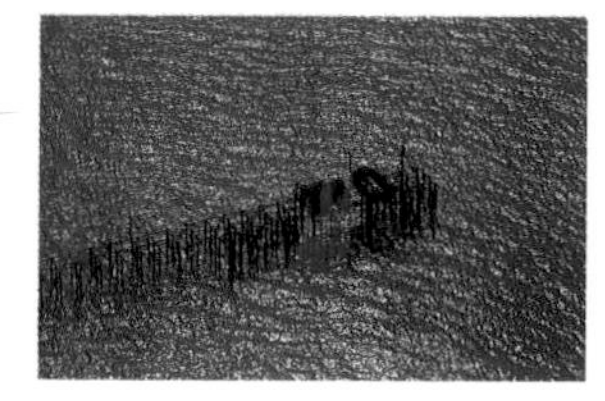

107. TONCHIGUE
A ruined dock, abandoned years ago, today makes an excellent apartment block for sea birds, suiting their needs as a place to stay the night or to build their nests.

108-109. POINT "LA BARCA"
The name of these shores translates as point of the boat. It happens That there is a shipwreck just there. It is difficult to know which came first, the name or the wreck.

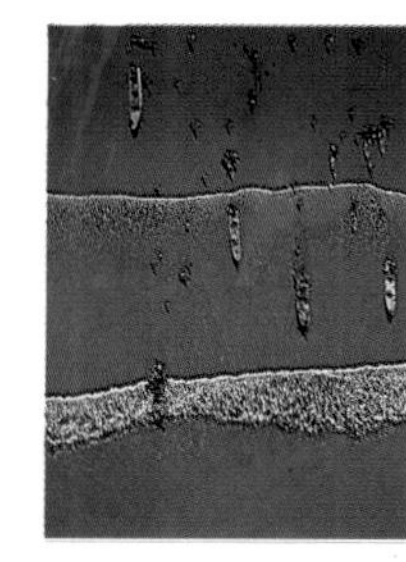

110. PUERTO LOPEZ
The people are going down to the beach from the village to meet the canoes arriving from the open sea. Early in the morning, it is time for the fish trade. There is a stain on the sand - the blood belonging to a turtle whose throat was cut. Turtles' blood has almost magic qualities and is drunk by everyone who can get hold of some.

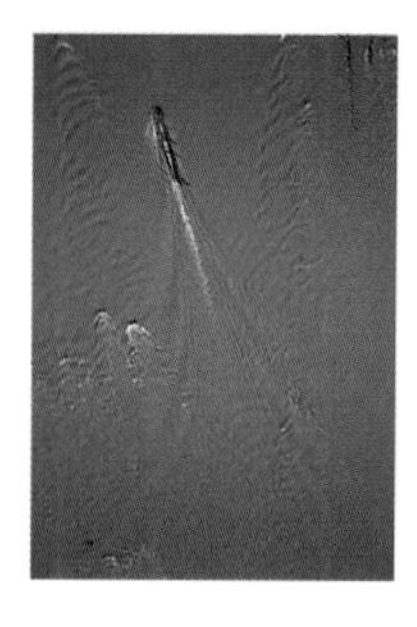

111 AGUARICO RIVER
Only recent are the roads making their way into the jungles of the amazon basin, before the only highways were the rivers.

112. TONCHIGUE
As the afternoon sun goes down, a father and son set out to sea to fish.

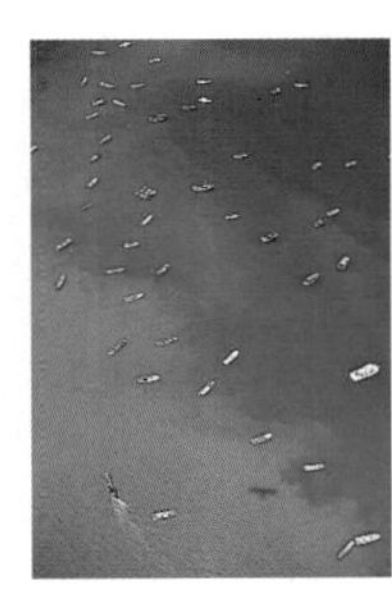

113. PUERTO LOPEZ
Small boats, canoes and "fibras" lie moored in the harbor of Puerto Lopez while their skippers rest. During winter, when it rains on the mountain, the adjacent river, the "Buena Vista" is loaded with sediment and the sea waters become two-tone.

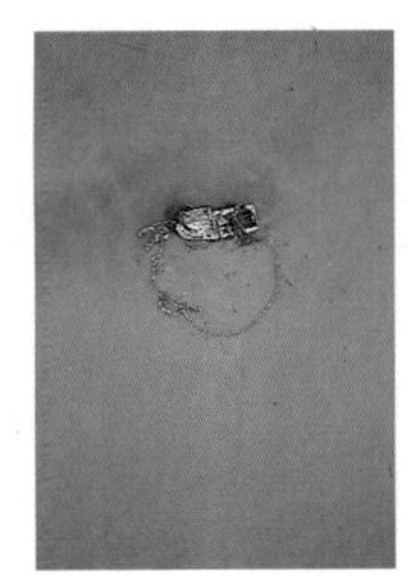

114. MANTA
The crew haul in the net that will eventually trap the fish. The pelicans, for their part, go ahead with the feast.

115. SALANGO
The pelicans on board or around the boat are looking for left-overs which are becoming less and less frequently available. With the problem of over-exploitation more technically advanced fishing fleets, the traditional fishermen face a difficult present and a cloudy future.

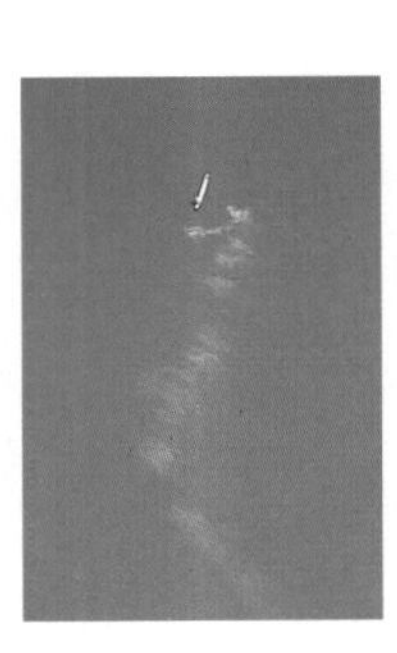

116. COJIMIES
A dissolving wake, made up of shrimp meal, is left behind the bongo.

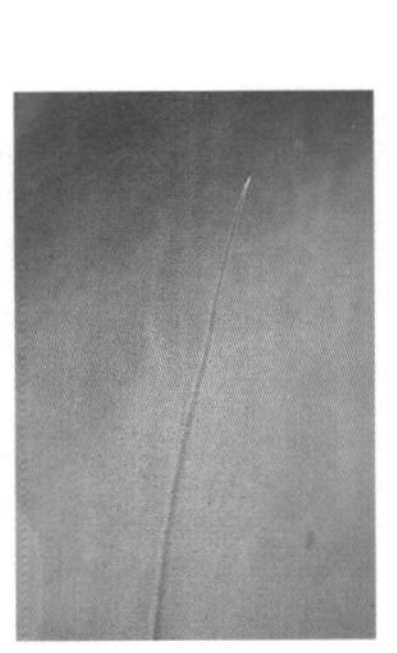

117. ESMERALDAS RIVER MOUTH
Outside the river mouth where the Esmeraldas spills into the Pacific, a canoe creates a blue wake. The waters of the river enter the sea loaded with sediment carried from the Andes, tainting several kilometers of water as they do so.

118-119. ATACAMES
This popular seaside resort is the destination of highlanders and foreigners alike. The former come to forget the cold of the Andean altitudes and the latter to forget the cold winter temperatures of other latitudes.

120. SALANGO
In Salango the waves break gently because it is protected by the islet. Hundreds of generations must have enjoyed such benefits; an assumption which is supported by the archeological remains of various different cultures that dot the landscape.

121. SUA
Súa has a spit of land which defends the small bay from the force of the Pacific. From its beaches children bathe unperturbed while the waves of Atacames, only a couple of kilometers away, are notoriously treacherous.

122-123. BAHIA DE CARAQUEZ
Clasping on to one another, as if fighting for the small beach where Bahia De Caraquez stands, are on one side the River Chone, and on the other the Pacific Ocean.

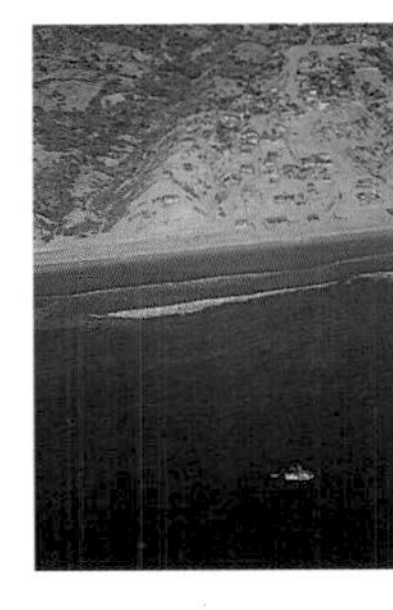

124. SAN JOSE
San Jose can be reached by car only through a dusty road and only in the dry season. The rest of the year the trip must be made by fishing boat.

125. ANCON
This is the northernmost town of the country, only a bit of sea and some mangroves separate it from Colombia. Ancon is inhabited mostly by blacks brougth from Africa a couple hundred years ago.

126-127. THE RIVER SUA
During the afternoon hours, when fishing is not good out at sea, the "fibras" remain moored in the shelter offered by the banks of the Súa.

128. LA BRAMADORA (THE BELLOWER)
A suggestive name for this settlement, still inhabited today by its founders who cleared the mountain of undergrowth But Ecuador is small and nowadays there is not much scope for new generations of colonists.

129. EL ESFUERZO (THE EFFORT)
The villages that have developed in what was once dense forest have names such as: "the Promising Future"; "Progress"; "Hope"; "Liberty"; "Victory" and "New world".

130-131. SANGOLQUI
Every Sunday the main square in Sangolqui fills with people. The awnings belong to the traders and the dots are mostly the heads or hats of shoppers, or the odd peddler who does not have the means to sell from an established stall.

132-133. SALINAS
Salinas is the beachresort of Guayaquil, on holidays the beaches are crowded by people in search of the sun and the waves, while the surrounding waters are sailed by boats fishing for black marlin.

134. MANTA
After Guayaquil there is a dispute between Manta and Machala as to which is the second most important port . Manta is mainly an entrance door, while through Machala great quantities of bananas and shrimps are exported,

135. GUAYAS RIVER
Just where the Babahoyo and the Daule rivers join to form the Guayas, stands the longest bridge of the country, it joins the city of Guayaquil with the inland cities.

136. CAHUASQUI
Cahuasqui appears to be isolated from the rest of the world as, apart from a few hectares of flat land, the village is surrounded on three sides by deep canyons and has high moorland behind it. The only access to the town is via a narrow, winding path which crosses the smallest of the canyons.

137. PABLO ARENAS
As if straddled on a hillside on the descending slopes of Cotacachi, is the village of Pablo Arenas. An isolated corner of the country where time seems to have stood still. The villagers say that here the only thing to have changed is the name - "before it had a better name", when it was called Cruz Cacho.

138. MURCO
Although small, the tiny village of Murco, at the foot of the Pasochoa Volcano, also has a modest church and a village square. The thing that stands out of the most in the photograph, however, is that they will soon be reaping an abundant maize harvest.

139. MACHACHI
The market takes place on the same day each week, it has different sites for the various products on offer. Here we can see the fruit and vegetable plaza, along with all the lorries needed to bring the produce to market.

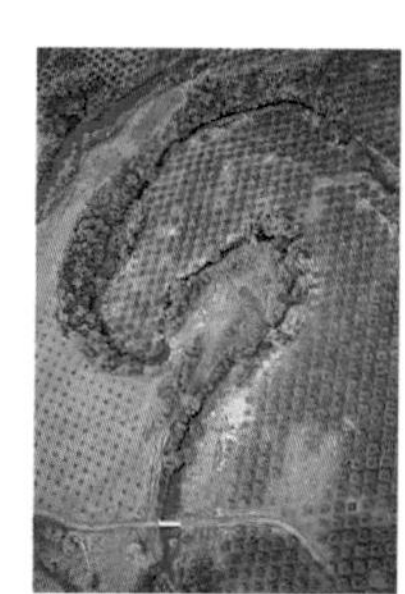

140. SALGANO RIVER
Aimless looks to be the meandering stream as it crosses the african palm plantation.

141. RIVER PROCEL
In the winter the streams of the coast flow rapidly between the green plains and the leafy trees. In the summer months, between June and December, the trees lose their leaves, the soil in the fields bears fruit, and the river-beds dry up.

142. RIVER CHONE
Scarcely visible, the bed of the Chone river-mouth is lost amongst the land flooded by the winter rains. The road between the cities of Chone and Bahia is built on a bank to save it from the problem of flooding.

143. RIVER GUAYLLABAMBA
The Guayllabamba is born in a small green nook of the Andes and dies in the middle of tropical vegetation in Esmeraldas, on its way passing through a deep canyon of walls and desert slopes.

144. PISQUE RIVER
All that can be farmed has been farmed up to the edge of the river canyon.

145. RIVER BUENA VISTA
With the heavy rainfalls of winter the river water becomes chocolate colored. In turn, the river itself will taint the part of the ocean into which it flows. During summer the river-bed dries up completely.

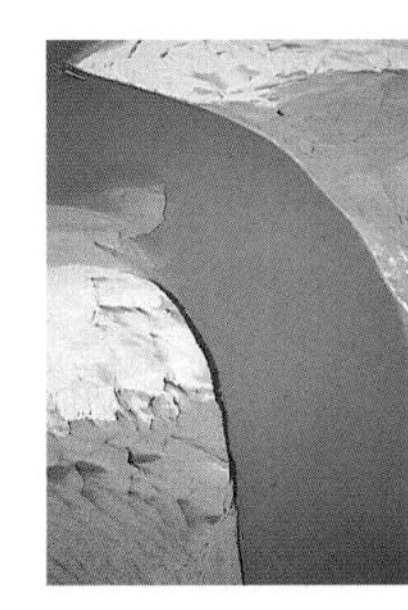

146. NAPO RIVER
Loaded with sediment carried from the high Andes, the color of the jungle rivers resembles a cup of milk with coffee. All that load ends fertilizing the jungle floor after the floods.

147. PANGAYACU
The Indian settlements in the Amazon basin are always located at the shore of a river. It is by the rivers that any of the few travelling goes on.

148-149. RIVER JATUN YACU
The Gran Rio (great river), as the name Jatun Yacu translates from Quichua to Spanish, descends hurriedly down the slopes of the Andes then opens up as it reaches the Amazonian plains.

150 LAGARTO RIVER
This meandering river is the border between Ecuador and Peru. Sometimes it course straightens or it bends even more, in this way giving and taking land to either of the two countries. It does so without taking in to account the wishes of neither the military or the foreing ministries of the two countries.

151 IMUYA
During the flood season the waters go out of its banks and inundate the jungle. Caymans and piranhas wander miles into the jungle in search of food.

152. RIVER AGUARICO
In the dawn light the jungle and the river Aguarico emerge beneath two thin cloaks of clouds.

153. PAÑACOCHA II
The Amazon basin has two important resources: one is called “black gold” and the other “green gold”. Underground the land is rich in oil and above it, in bio-diversity. The first resource must be extracted with care not to loose the second one.

154. SAN VICENTE
Whenever the tide permits, the “chivas” or “rancheras” take a short cut along the beach, always smoother than the roads inland. First class, with an exceptional view and access to the sun, is on the roof. One can try to change seats or class even when the vehicle is in motion.

OCEANO PACIFICO
89 121 126
92 107 112
86 118
117
98 103
93 104 116 96
125
48 84 10 32 136 137 78
34 35
76 44
62 63
95 142
64 140 40
12 129
97 154
128
143 6 56 57
194 144 22
66 138 70 139
79 53 23
27 8 67
94 122 18
47
26 28
114 134
46
108 102 124
55 59 73 74 54
33 31
49 50
5 145
100 110 113 115 120 16
69 67 68 65 45
30 24
52
105 61 141 14 75
87 88
77
132 135 90 80